The Wounded Soldier

Sandy Davis Kirk, Ph.D.

The Wounded Soldier
by Sandy Davis Kirk, Ph.D.

Copyright © 2015

No part of this book may be reproduced or transmitted in any form or by any means, electronic, or mechanical, including photocopying, recording, or by any information storage and retrieval system, without the written permission from the author.

All rights reserved.

ISBN 978-1506105529

Published by The Indie Authors' Guild

For more information about independent author publishing email: vince@theindieauthors.com

Contents

Dedication 1

One: The Wounded Soldier 2

Two: The Soldier's Hope 11

Three: A Soldier's Grief 23

Four: A Soldier Forgives 33

Five: The Soldier's Hell 41

Six: The Lonely Soldier 49

Seven: A Soldier's Scars 55

Eight: The Soldier's Homecoming 65

Nine: The Greatest Soldier 75

Dedication

Dedicated to all the brave men and women who have served in the Armed Forces of the United States of America:

When I saw you in your uniform, dressed for battle, it took my breath away. When I tried to thank you for your service, my words stuck in my throat. When I looked into your eyes and saw your courage tinged with fear, my heart stood still for I knew what you faced ahead. And when I saw your wounds as you returned home, I wept inside with unspeakable gratitude. I still continue to weep for your heroic sacrifice.

"This is how we know what love is: Jesus Christ laid down his life for us. And we ought to lay down our lives for our brothers."
1 John 3:16

Chapter One:
The Wounded Soldier

He knows the feeling of a tear...

One terrifying thought fills the soldier's mind. What will she think when she sees my face? As a prisoner of war in a German prison camp, Private Joe's face had been horribly burned. Often in his cell, with pain racking his body, especially his face which had been burned beyond recognition, loneliness engulfed him. He would think of his family and especially the girl he loved and hoped to marry. Finally, the Germans released him and he was returned as a war hero.

Now he stands, dressed in crisp uniform, his back to the audience as he and several others receive the Distinguished Service Cross. As the medal is pinned upon his jacket, paralyzing fears flood his thoughts. He hears only bits and phrases of the praise heaped upon him: "For extraordinary heroism against the enemy . . . with complete disregard for his own safety . . . reflects great credit on himself and the Armed Forces. . . ."

He had begged, even ordered, his girlfriend not to come. He wanted to wait until enough plastic surgeries had been performed that she could bear to look at his face. But she never promised, and now he wonders if somewhere out there in the sea of people gathered for the ceremony could be the one he loves.

The ceremony ends and people shake the hero's hand, but he hardly notices. His eyes scan restlessly, searching, longing. Then suddenly three people break from the crowd— Joe's parents and his girlfriend. She smiles broadly as she runs toward him on the platform. Instinctively, almost forgetting his face, he races toward her.

They meet in the middle of the auditorium. Hundreds of eyes watch, but the two are unaware. The girl looks straight into Joe's flaming red, malformed face. She never flinches. Throwing her arms around him, she cries over and over again, "Joe! Joe! Joe! You are the most beautiful man in the whole world!" (i)

Now in this book, I want to tell you about another Wounded Soldier, the most beautiful man who ever lived. Though His "appearance was so disfigured beyond that of any man and his form marred beyond human likeness," (ii) His countenance is stunning. And though physical wounds normally heal with time, even now, as He sits at the right hand of

God in heaven, He still bears deep, gaping wounds from His sacrifice.

In these pages, I want to paint a picture before your eyes. It's a graphic description of the One who was wounded beyond recognition. Though He is God, He came in human flesh so that He could know the feeling of a tear slipping down His cheek. There were no tears or pain in heaven, and He wanted to know the raw ache of loneliness and the excruciating pain of being mortally wounded.

Just like you, He was willing to lay down His life for His brothers and sisters. He came all the way from heaven so that He could be with you in your times of deepest pain. In the midst of the firestorm of war, He wants to be your refuge.

That's why it means so much to me to put this little book in your hands. Every time I pass a soldier in an airport, I can feel the tears welling up in my heart like a great ocean wave. And when I open my mouth to try to express my thankfulness, the wave always breaks and I burst out in tears. I can't help it. My heart is so full of gratitude to you young men and women who are laying your lives on the line for our freedom.

When I am finally able to talk through the tears, thanking you for your service, I always wish I could give you something to express my appreciation. Now, at last, I can give you this book from my heart. I've authored many books, but none has touched my emotions so deeply as this one. It's because of your heroic sacrifice.

So please accept this gift and allow it to give you deep comfort in the days to come. Many challenges lay ahead for you. Some of you will go to battle and see horrifying scenes of blood and pain and war that will haunt you. You may be wounded yourself, possibly wounded beyond recognition. Some of you may even pay the ultimate price.

That's why I'm asking you to pull aside from your grueling schedule to read these pages. If you will, I promise you will find the simple, yet infinitely profound answer to your secret fears and your deepest questions about life.

A former slave lifted up her little girl, as a train, carrying the flag-draped casket of the fatally wounded Abraham Lincoln, passed by. "Take a long look, Honey!" she cried. "That's the man who died to set you free!" (iii) This is what we will do in this book. We will take a long steady look at the Wounded Soldier, who died to set us free. It will be a life changing gaze. As someone has said, "Since my eyes were fixed on Jesus, I've lost sight of all beside; so enchained my spirit's vision, gazing on the Crucified." (iv)

So I offer you this little book, inviting you to come and behold the most beautiful man in the world. Come see the one man on earth who knows what real sacrifice is like. Gaze into His eyes, swollen from blows to His face, bloodshot from sleeplessness. Please don't look away. Don't hide your eyes from the grinding pain of the cross.

Though it may hurt to look, it will heal the wounds in your soul. Don't think, because He was God enfleshed in human skin, that He didn't feel pain. He chose to place himself in the same human flesh you have. He could feel every slash of the scourge, every rip of tissue and nerves, every drop of seeping blood, but He did it all for you.

That's why no one understands like Jesus. He knows the sacrifice you have made to be a soldier in the military, for He is the ultimate Wounded Soldier.

Chapter One End Notes:

(i) Adapted from the true story by I. Kaufman, condensed from American Jews in World War II; cited in Jack Canfield, Mark Victor Hansen and Sidney R. Slagter, compilers, "The Most Beautiful Man in the World," Chicken Soup for the Veteran's Soul (Deerfield Beach, FL: Health Communications, Inc., 2001), pp. 237-241.

(ii) Isaiah 53:14

(iii) Jeffrey O'Leary, America Out of the Ashes, Janet Chismar, "God Returns to America's Public Square," (Honor Books, 2001), p. 205.

(iv) Walter B. Knight, Masterbook of New Illustrations (Grand Rapids, MI: William B. Eerdmans Publishing Company, 1956), p. 722.

Chapter Two: The Soldier's Hope

"If you will save me, I will serve you forever!"– Louis Zamperini

On a faraway battlefield a young soldier lies severely wounded. As his lifeblood soaks into the ground, he keeps thinking, *Oh, God, I'm dying. I'm not ready to meet you. Help me, Lord!*

With his head pressed down in the mud, he feels his own warm blood pooling around his face. Over and over in his mind, he thinks, *What was that Bible verse my grandfather always told me? "Someday, Son, you'll have to get right with God. When that time comes, remember this verse: 'The blood of Jesus cleanses you from all unrighteousness. . . for if you confess your sins, He is faithful and just to forgive your sin and cleanse you.'"*[1]

Yes! Yes, that was it! Now, even as the life force drains out, he cries out to God, confessing his sin and asking the blood of Jesus to cleanse him. Peace fills his heart, and he relaxes, losing consciousness. Days later the soldier awakens in a hospital, surprised to be alive. A medic had found him and lifted him by helicopter to safety. Now, as he regains his strength, he knows he is a changed man. Christ has come into his life, even as he was almost dying. He feels free and pure, a new creation in Christ.

Oh, sure, maybe this was what some call a "fox-hole conversion," but it was still real. That young soldier had been forgiven and the blood of Jesus had washed him perfectly clean. If you need forgiveness, His blood will do the same for you.

Maybe you've seen the true story of Louie Zamperini in the movie

"Unbroken." But I want to tell you the part of the story the movie didn't show. When Louie returned home from several years of suffering as a prisoner of war (P.O.W.) in Japan, memories haunted him day and night. His insides raged with bitterness toward the Japanese. With fierce anger, he hated a man called "the Bird," whose driving goal was to break this Olympic track star and grind him into nothing. Back in America, flashbacks, fits of rage, and nightmares with brutal scenes of the Bird, tormented him nightly.

Louie began drinking to numb the memories until finally he was a full on alcoholic. One night he awakened, dreaming he was choking "the Bird," but actually he was choking his beautiful young wife, Cynthia. On the verge of divorcing him, and as a last resort, she drug him into a tent meeting in Los Angeles where a young evangelist named Billy Graham was just starting out in ministry.[1]

Now the tall young evangelist stepped up to the microphone. With trembling authority, he began laying out the gospel. He told about hell and salvation, about being saved or lost. He said, "God takes down your life from the time you were born to the time you die.... They are going to pull down a screen and they are going to shoot the moving picture of your life from the cradle to the grave, and you are going to hear every thought that was going through your mind every minute of the day, every second of the minute, and you're going to hear the words that you said. And your own words, and your own thoughts, and your own deeds are going to condemn you as you stand before God on that day...."

Graham looked out over his audience. "Here tonight, there's a drowning man, a drowning woman. . . ." Louie grew angrier by the moment. And when Graham said, "Every head bowed and every eye closed," offering an invitation to repent and receive Christ, Louie grabbed his wife's hand and shoved his way out of the tent. That night his dreams were unbearably tormenting.

The next day his wife pleaded with her husband to come with her again. Louie finally gave in with one caveat. When Graham calls people to close their eyes and bow their heads, they were leaving.

That night under the tent Graham began describing the flaming fingertip of God, who created the universe, and left his footprints in the stars that sprinkle the skies. The description caused Louie's thoughts to slip back to another harrowing night under the stars which sparkled over the Pacific Ocean.

Five years before, Louie and two other airmen had survived the crash of their plane into the vast expanse of the ocean. They lay slowly dying in a life raft underneath that starry sky. As sharks circled hungrily around them, Japanese war planes occasionally peppered them with bullets, and their bodies wasted away from starvation and thirst, they had no hope of survival. One of his crewmates died and they had to drop his body overboard. But suddenly, a Japanese ship showed up and the two survivors were taken to a prisoner of war camp in Japan. The torture there was unthinkable.

Graham's words broke through again. "What God asks of men is faith. His invisibility is the truest test of that faith."[1]

His words struck Louie's heart. He felt a frantic urge to flee. Graham continued, "Now with every head bowed and every eye closed...."

Hot fury rose inside Louie. He seized his wife's hand and began pushing through the people on his row. He felt enraged, violent, and wanting to hit someone. As he reached the aisle, suddenly another memory flooded his mind. He saw himself again on that raft in the Pacific. He was dying of thirst, but he lifted his face toward heaven and through swollen lips, he heard himself whisper, "If you will save me, I will serve you forever."

Graham then said boldly, "God has spoken to you now, so come...." Louie's heart stood still. He knew in that moment that he had made a long-forgotten promise to God which he had never kept. He turned around and made his way forward to receive Jesus Christ as his Lord and Savior. That night he rushed straight home and poured out gallons of liquor. He gathered his stash of cigarettes and girlie magazines and heaved them into the trash.

After that, Louie never had another flashback or nightmare. "The Bird" never invaded his dreams again. He awakened the next morning knowing he was free—a completely new creation.[1]

If you feel like Louie, knowing you need forgiveness, will you do the most important thing you've ever done in your whole life? You may be facing some huge battles in the days and months to come, and you need to know you are ready to meet your God. His one and only Son, who lived with Him before the creation of the world, has come to save you. To give you a new life and to help you know you have eternal life with Him.

So right now, come to the only place on this planet where true salvation can be found. Come to that lowly hill where the blood of God spilled down upon this earth. Come to the foot of the cross and look up at Jesus Christ. Look into his face, and hear Him whisper, through cracked and bleeding lips, "Father, forgive them...."

Then watch the blood dripping down from the thorns which smashed and pierced into his skull. See the dark red droplets clotting in His hair, seeping down into his eyes and nose and beard, and dripping down His throat. That blood has the innate power to cleanse you. It holds the DNA of God. He only waits for you to tell Him you are sorry, genuinely sorry, and that you want to give your life to Him.

Please don't wait until your life is imploding like Louie's life was. Jesus said that we must become like a little child if we want to enter the kingdom of God. So be willing to humble yourself, and admit your need for a Savior. Ask Jesus Christ to come live inside your spirit by saying something like this:

Jesus, I confess to you that I am a sinner. I am so sorry for all the things I've said and done that were not pure in your sight. I'm sorry that I have resisted you all these years. (Take a few moments to confess to Him the worst things you've ever done, and if tears of repentance come, let them freely flow for they will touch the heart of God).

Please forgive me and wash me clean in your blood. Right now, I open my heart and ask you to come live inside me. Come, Lord Jesus. I surrender my life to you. I admit my need for you in my life. I give you everything. I submit my will and my heart to you. Come and live your life in me. (Keep praying in your own words until you know He has come to fill you with himself).

Now how do you feel? I think you feel fresh and clean like a new creation. This is what it means to be born again. To be forgiven. This is the Soldier's greatest hope.

And now, no matter what you go through on the battlefield of war or the trenches of life, you can know—really know—that you are saved. Like that soldier dying in the mud in the opening story of this chapter, the blood of Jesus has washed you clean. And like Louie Zamperini, the Spirit of Christ has made you a new man or woman. It's all because you have surrendered to Christ. You have been forgiven and washed in the blood of *the Wounded Soldier.*

Chapter Three: A Soldier's Grief

"I cannot get over his death!"

"Doc, we have a man down!" came the voice on the phone. Clint, a Navy Corpsman who had been sent to the frontline to care for fallen Marines, wondered which one of his Marines it could be. He asked the gunny, "Can you get me over to that injured Marine?" He replied, "No, we are taking too much fire and there are vehicles in the way."

So with the enemy in plain sight and sniper fire and rocket propelled grenades exploding all around him, Clint dared to race to the side of the wounded soldier. When he got to him, his heart filled his throat. It was one of his best friends! He looked at his friend and he knew it was serious.

Blood spurted out from a wound in the right side of his neck. Clint did everything he could, from dressing his wound to suctioning out blood from his mouth by sucking it out with his own mouth. But he couldn't save him. His friend died in his arms, and Clint was devastated.

After he laid his friend's lifeless body down, he went to the other side of the Hummer and threw up. "I felt the air fill with sadness that hot dusty day in Iraq," Clint said, "and I knew my life would never be the same."[1]

Oh, if only I could have a few moments with those of you who feel just like Clint. I could never help you myself, but through the years I have discovered a secret to finding relief from traumatic experiences. The secret is getting the buried grief out. And the place of healing is on an ancient hill where the blood of God dripped down for wounded hearts.

If I could say one thing to you, it would be this—please let all your grief pour out on Jesus. I've ministered to hundreds of young adults, and I have always found that the deepest healing comes when they let the grief spill out at the foot of the cross.

I learned this by getting my own grief out. That's when my life changed from depression to overflowing joy. This is easier for us girls, but for you men, it is so hard to do. Guys were told, "Big boys don't cry!" so they stuff the emotions down inside until the feelings harden into a rock. Sometimes you can feel the raw ache inside, or sometimes the ache turns numb. It causes you not to feel much of anything anymore.

That's why I'm asking you—if you have suffered any kind of trauma or pain, whether on the battlefield or from broken relationships in life, please look up again at Jesus Christ.

Look until you can see the tears pooling in His eyes and swimming down His cheeks. Gaze at Him until you can almost reach up and touch the nails quivering in His hands. Until you can almost feel the wet drops of blood pouring from open wounds.

Then tell Him how you feel. Talk to Him out loud. Expose to Him the worst thing that has happened to you. Describe to Him what you saw. I know it hurts to talk about it, but you need to get this out. And remember— no one understands like Jesus.

Tell Him about the soldier dying in your arms. Convey to Him about your best friend dying. Expose to Him how you felt about the blood that caused you to wretch. Disclose to Him the terrifying scene, whatever it was.

Communicate to Him what hurt or shocked you the most.

Then let Him walk into that grisly memory. Let Him hold you close and comfort you, like a loving Father. Even if your own dad wasn't there for you, He will be the strong, protective, loving Father you have always needed. Try to let the grief pour out in liquid tears, like a baby crying in his or her daddy's arms.

Let the tears roll out on Him, and when the tears are dried, let Him flood you with His love. Like a dry sponge soaking up fresh water, let His love infuse your whole being. It's the love of the One who "carried our griefs"[1] to the cross and knows the feeling of tears washing His face and soaking into His beard.

I was teaching in a Bible school in Canada, when the leader of the school asked if he could see me privately. He told me that he could not seem to get over the death of his father, who had been tragically killed in a farming accident. I asked, "James, what is it about your father's death that hurts you the most?"

I know this question is painfully probing, but I wanted to help him get to the bottom of his deepest grief. He immediately burst out, "Because he will never get to meet Heidi and he won't be at our wedding!" He fell to the floor sobbing, and I knelt down, placing my hand on his back. I encouraged him to let out all the grief. "Let the dam break. Don't hold anything back. Pour it all out on Jesus." He did, and when he got off that floor, he was ready to be filled back up with the Holy Spirit. We asked the Lord to fill him, and the Spirit of God came down so strongly that, like the believers at Pentecost, he was like a drunk man![1]

This is the power of getting grief out. There's much more to being healed, which we will see in the following chapters, but this is where it begins, for no one understands like Jesus.[1]

It's like the soldier who lay in a hospital bed, his arm blown off in Afghanistan. Anger and pain so engulfed him that he would not talk to anyone, not even family. His pastor heard about it and flew to be with him in the hospital, but the wounded young man refused to see him.

Despite his resistance, the pastor entered his room and stood patiently waiting. The soldier knew he was there but he kept his back to him, his face to the wall. Finally in disgust the young man turned over and looked at his pastor. What he saw took his breath away. He gasped and shot straight up, tears filling his eyes.

The pastor stood with his pant legs rolled up, exposing a prosthesis attached to each of his thighs. His own legs had been blown off in another war, but the boy never knew it. The older man walked over to the soldier's bed, sat down, and slipped his arm around him. The young man fell on his chest, sobbing. "I understand what you're going through, Son," said the pastor. "I really understand."

After the young man poured out his tears, the pastor said one more thing. "Son, if you feel like I did, you may have been blaming God for what happened to you." The young man nodded.

"You probably didn't even realize you've been mad at God, but Jesus said, 'The thief comes only to kill and steal and destroy; but I have come that they may have life, and have it to the full.'[1] Jesus didn't do this to you, Son. The thief did."

As a soldier, you may have some harrowing experiences ahead. You may see things that others never see, but please remember—you have a refuge. It's the cross of Jesus Christ. Run back to His bleeding feet and tell Him all about it.

And remember, Jesus didn't do this to you. You may need to say something like this, "Jesus, I'm sorry, I've been blaming you for what happened to me."

Tell Him how you feel, and when the tears of grief and sorrow have spilled out on Him, then lift your face to heaven. Ask Him to fill you back up with the Holy Spirit. Let Him breathe His sweet Spirit into the hole in your soul. He will help you feel again.

So no matter what you go through in the cold war of life or the battlefield of war, cling to the cross of Christ. Like no one else in all the world, Jesus understands, for He is the compassionate *Wounded Soldier.*

Chapter Four: A Soldier Forgives

When revenge eats you up inside

"May I repent to you, Sir, for the terrible things my Japanese people did to you in the prison camp?" said Ikue, a Japanese student at our internship in Alabama.

Her words took eighty-two year old Colonel Glenn Frazier, a former P.O.W., by surprise. He sat down, shaken. He could see the tears rimming her eyes and sliding down her cheeks.

"May I humble myself to you and wash your feet as a way of showing you my deep sorrow for what my people did to you?" Her words melted his heart and suddenly memories from the torturous years in the filthy prison camps of the Philippines and Japan flooded into his mind.

As warm water, mingled with Ikue's tears, poured over his feet, he thought of the Bataan Death March during which, for seven grueling days and nights he walked until his feet bled, his stomach ached for food, and his tongue was swollen from thirst. He thought of all the merciless beatings, the starvation of living on one small bowl of rice a day, filled with live squirming worms. He thought of the hatred and rage and revenge he held toward all Japanese people.

When the war finally ended and Colonel Glenn was released from the suffering, he returned home to a joyful family reunion. But tormenting dreams haunted his sleep and the rage in his heart grew wilder by the day. Because of the mental torture, he moved from job to job and marriage to broken marriage.

Finally, he realized he had to forgive, and he cried out to God to help him. Slowly he was able to forgive his enemy and live again. But still, it was so hard to completely forgive where there had been no genuine apology.

Now here was this young Japanese student, kneeling down and weeping over his pain. "I am so sorry for all the beatings. . . the cruelty. . . all the starving. . . "cried Ikue, her heart in her words. Suddenly, Glen broke. He wept and wept and he forgave with all his heart. To this day, his wife Terri tells me, "That was one of the greatest experiences of my husband's life!" Colonel Glenn told me, "An apology from the Emperor of Japan could not have meant so much to me!"

That was the day all pain and anger and rage washed away like logs on a downstream river. Just like Colonel Glenn, God wants to do the same in you. He wants to free you from all the hidden bitterness and rage, especially the hatred toward your enemy.

So come again to look up at *the Wounded Soldier.* Look even deeper than the pain and wounds and blood. Look at what happened to Him spiritually. Picture the scene on that hill outside Jerusalem...

Suddenly, the sky turns dark as night. A sense of terror sweeps down over Jesus. He thrashes and writhes as though something gruesome has fallen upon Him. His eyes bulge with fear. Tears swim down His face as He convulses in terror. The wounds on His back tear open and soak the wood of the cross with His blood.

What is happening to Jesus? Even the crowd stands mute with shock. His own mother hides her face from the horrific scene. But what is this? Do you know?[1]

Right now, God the Father has opened heaven and poured down upon His own beloved Son the sins of all humanity. All the murder and hatred and bitterness and rage, all the lust and perversion and pornography and rape and fornication—flood down on the innocent One. All the pride and self-pity and greed and gossip and slander and all the sins of humanity smash down on the pure Lamb of God.

Think about your worst sins—no matter what they are—they poured down on Him. Pause and think about it. . . Imagine your sin on Him. Picture your worst sexual sin emptied into the Wounded One. See your drugs and alcohol addictions, and what these substances made you do to others, all plunged down on Him. He takes it all into himself. That's why, there on the cross, the Bible says, "He became sin."[1]

But it's not just your sin. It's the sin of your enemy as well. Now Jesus turns to you and says, "Forgive your enemy as I have forgiven you." If you don't forgive, the poison of bitterness will eat you up on the inside. It will hold you in a prison of torment.

"But I'm not the perpetrator. I'm the victim!" you might be thinking. "He's the one who should repent, not me!" Yes, but resentment is still sin and it stands between you and God. He will wash you clean when you acknowledge your sin, confessing sin as sin. So look back up at Jesus and tell Him, "I am sorry for all my hatred, my anger, my bitterness and rage. Please wash me and cleanse me of this sin." Say it to God until you know you really mean it. He can see your heart.

And now it's time to forgive, but you cannot do it in your own strength. You need help. So ask the Holy Spirit to come and give you the power to forgive. Whisper something like this: "Holy Spirit, I am powerless to forgive, but I ask you to come and give me the grace, the strength and ability to forgive. Come Holy Spirit..."

Wait a few minutes until He comes. And then, still picturing Jesus, say, "With your power, I forgive _____." Then see yourself lifting up your enemy and placing him or her on the cross. Say to the Lord, "I give my enemy to you, and I sincerely bless him." With all your heart keep releasing and blessing him or her until you know it's done.

Then, with your eyes still on Jesus, once more ask the Holy Spirit to come and fill you back up. "Come, Holy Spirit. Come and fill me...." Open wide your heart and receive the Holy Spirit. Breathe Him in. Let Him fill and fill and fill, making you into a Soldier whose heart is completely free. Rage has dissolved and fresh joy is flooding your life.

Now immerse yourself every day in the Holy Spirit and in daily Bible reading as Jesus makes you into a strong man or woman, healed of rage, and filled with the glory of the *Wounded Soldier* himself.

Chapter Five: The Soldier's Hell

"He could never forgive me for what I've done!"

Corporal Jason Dunham patrolled the Syrian border in April 2004, when suddenly an enemy soldier jumped him and grabbed him around the neck. They struggled in the dirt, and then Jason saw a live grenade fall from the man's hand. Rather than allowing his company of men to be blown up, Jason threw his helmet over the grenade, wrapped his arms around it and held it down.

Then came the explosion. When the smoke cleared, Jason's helmet was shredded and he lay face down in a pool of blood. He died a few months later, having given his life to save his men.[1]

In an even higher way, that's what Jesus Christ did for you. He threw himself upon the grenade of wrath that would explode over you. He took the hell that you deserve for sin—on *himself!* Did you know that He did this for you? He couldn't bear to see you suffer in hell, so He took it on himself. He was punished for you.

John the Baptist pointed to Jesus and cried, "Behold the Lamb who takes away the sin of the world!" [1] But how did He take away sin? Do you know?

Oh, the answer will cause your heart to tremble. I know my heart has never stopped shaking since I learned this fathomless truth. I had cried more tears over the death of my dog than over the death of my Lord—until I learned about the Father's cup of wrath. Now I've been teaching it and writing books on it for almost thirty years.[1] So look back up at Jesus to see what happened next...

Jesus has been thrashing and writhing under the terrible weight of human sin. But now His body suddenly stiffens. His face pales and He turns rigid. He lifts His eyes toward heaven. See the horror in His eyes. He sees it coming... What is it? This is the Father's cup. This is the cup He prayed about in the garden, which caused blood to squeeze from the pores of His skin. It is the storm of God's wrath roaring down in wave after wave after wave of punishment.

Why is God exploding His wrath down on His own beloved Son? Because God is punishing Him in your place. It's not that God is cruel and vindictive. It's that sin has infused the human race, and sin cannot come into the presence of a holy God. So Jesus takes it for you. All the wrath and judgment that you and I deserve for sin are tumbling down on Him. He is being punished in your place.

You may say, "I deserve hell for all the things I've done!" But look at Jesus. He endures hell as your substitute. Like the soldier who took the full explosion of the grenade to save his men, that's what Jesus did for you! He braved the flames of hell on the cross for you so that you could be with Him forever.

Oh, why did He do it? There is one huge reason. Jesus saw what would happen if He didn't step in and take your hell upon himself. He saw you burning in the flames of hell, and he could not bear it. He wanted you to be with Him forever in eternity. Can you believe He loves you so much? He took hell so that you could have His heaven.

"But you don't know what I've done!" you might be saying. That's what Brian said to me one night. "I deserve hell for what I've done," he said. Horrifying memories tormented him night and day because of a traumatic experience as a boy. Finally, he groaned, "When I was eight, my dad made me hold a gun and shoot a man in the head. I had to see the blood and brains splattered across the room and watch him die! God could never forgive me for that!"

I knew my words couldn't heal Brian's heart. He needed to go to the cross. We have a huge cross in our chapel, so I took him over to it. I asked him to close his eyes and picture Jesus Christ. I told him to see all of his sin—the murder, the hatred toward his father, the fear, the drugs—see it all laid down upon the Lamb.

Then I told him to imagine Jesus, infused with sin, as the wrath of hell burns down upon him. "This is your hell, Brian! This is what you deserve for sin, but your Lord Jesus took it for you. He was punished in your place!"

Brian was stunned. He never knew that Jesus had taken his punishment on the cross. I said, "Brian, I'm sure you've told him how sorry you are a thousand times before, but tell Him now—in the presence of God—and He will wash you clean."

Brian began telling God he was sorry. Then the dam broke and he wept and wept in gut-wrenching sobs of repentance. It was powerful because repentance is like the doorway to God. When we repent with "tears of godly sorrow," turning away from sin with all our heart, something inside softens and opens up.[1]

Finally Brian lifted his head and faintly smiled. He knew he was forgiven, but now the hardest part was forgiving himself. So I asked him to do something that I knew would help him forgive himself. The eyes are the window to the soul, so I held a mirror in front of his eyes and asked him to say, "Because Jesus has forgiven me, I forgive myself." He said it until it went into his soul, and he knew he was forgiven.

I cannot tell you the freedom that came to that young man. He laughed. He cried, and the Holy Spirit filled him so full he was bubbling over with joy. He could barely walk he was so inebriated with God. He came into our chapel, guilty and heavily weighed down with torment, but he left brimming with the Holy Spirit.

Though other young adults of your generation are out there drinking, and partying, and getting smashed, and mocking the things of God, you are not so shallow. You know you cannot afford to play games with life and death. Your life is on the line. You could be facing impending death tomorrow.

Maybe you already knew that Jesus drank the Father's cup of wrath on the cross, but you can bet, your brothers and sisters in your company don't know it. They need to know what Jesus did for them. Only those who surrender to Him and receive Him as their Lord can receive His forgiveness. Will you tell them? Or will you at least hand them this little book and let them read it for themselves?

They need to know how much God loves them. They need to know that God's own Son took their place and was punished for their sin. They need to know this timeless truth: so that they could have forgiveness, their hell was engulfed by God's own *Wounded Soldier.*

Chapter Six:
The Lonely Soldier

"Why has God forsaken me?"

Dave Roever, one of America's heroes from Vietnam, tells the heartbreaking story of a man near his bed in the hospital. Every inch of his skin had been burned and blown off in the war. Bandages covered him from head to toe.

One day the soldier's young wife came into the hospital room to visit him. She took one look at her husband and was sickened. She callously pulled off her wedding ring and flipped it onto the bed. "I couldn't walk down the street with you," she said cruelly. "You're embarrassing!"

The soldier was crushed. He felt utterly forsaken by the woman he loved. This is the girl who filled his thoughts and dreams during his loneliest moments in Vietnam. Her memory was what kept him alive. But after this heartless rejection, a few days later he died.[1]

This heart-wrenching true story sadly displays the sense of forsakenness that so many soldiers feel, especially those who are wounded beyond recognition. But also, many soldiers, returning from war, are so traumatized (PTSD) that they cannot function in American society. They experience a certain kind of loneliness that no one can truly understand, except for God himself.

So come again to the hill of Calvary and look up at the lonely, twisted, bleeding figure on the cross....

As it nears the ninth hour, or 3:00 o'clock in the afternoon, Jesus pushes down hard on the spike in His feet, lifting His chest to take in a lungful of air. This sudden thrust on the spike, rips open the wounds in His feet. Blood spurts from beneath the spike, spilling down His feet and toes, dripping down the wood of the cross and soaking into the ground.

Jesus turns His gaze upward. Tears quiver in His eyes. He throws back His head His mouth flies open wide as though He's about to speak. He spoke three times in the first three hours, once to forgive, next to save a dying thief, and third to place His mother in the care of John, the young disciple.

In these last three hours, not a word has fallen from His lips. The pain has been too deep for words. The horror of drinking the Father's cup of wrath has crushed His breath away. Now, however, He prepares to speak.

The crowd hushes. John and Mary inch in a little closer. For a moment, time stands still. Tension crackles in the air. The atmosphere thickens. Hearts thunder in every breast.

Now, with a deep, guttural, animal-like roar, Jesus shrieks, "*Eli, Eli, lama sabachthani?*" The words are a mixture of Hebrew and Aramaic. They mean, "My God, My God, why have you forsaken me?"[1]

The multitude at Calvary stands paralyzed. Birds' songs freeze mid-air. The wind holds its breath. The sun still hides its face. Dark clouds, heavy with moisture, hang low as though ready to drop a load of tears.[1]

Jesus' words thunder across the hillside. When the Roman scourge plowed open His flesh, thorns pierced His brow like icepicks, spikes drove through His hands and feet, and people spat up in His face, He remained silent: "As a sheep before her shearers is silent, so he did not open his mouth."[1]

Yet now, He screams like a wounded animal. He doesn't whimper like a lamb; He roars like a lion. Do you know why?

It is not because of the horror of taking God's wrath, as terrifying as that was. It was because He had to bear that punishment alone. God's presence lifted from Him during His time of greatest need. But why? The answer speaks volumes to every lonely soldier who has ever laid his or her life on the line.

Jesus plumbed the deepest pit of human agony for you. He was abandoned by God so that you would never be abandoned by God. He was deserted so that you would never be deserted.

No matter what you go through in the lonely trenches of military life, He promises that He will be there with you. He will never abandon you. He says, "Never will I leave you; never will I forsake you."[1] He suffered loneliness to the uttermost so that He could comfort you when you are lonely.

So remember, the hand that wipes your tears is scarred. The One who is always there to comfort you, was forsaken so that you would never be alone. He is your best friend, your faithful Father, your *Wounded Soldier.*

Chapter Seven: A Soldier's Scars

His wounds tell the story

In a little village in Korea, an American soldier ambled down the road when suddenly he looked up to see a house burning. He could hear screams for help coming from inside the inferno so he broke through a window and gathered up two children lying unconscious on the floor.

As he bent down to pick up the two little ones, the roof caved in and he was terribly burned on his face and neck and hands. Due to his daring rescue, the children survived but they were now orphans, for their parents died in the flames. They were brought to America where they were put up for adoption, and the soldier was shipped home to recover from his burn wounds.

Several months later, a judge in America held a hearing to review the cases of various applicants who wanted to adopt the children. He listened as each couple told why they deserved to adopt the children into their family. Then he turned to a young soldier, who had returned from the war and had applied to adopt them as well.

"Young man," the judge said skeptically, "what makes you think you deserve to adopt these children?"

The soldier didn't say a word. He simply stood, pulled open the collar on his shirt, then held up both hands. A gasp filled the courtroom as everyone saw his scarred hands and face and neck. Then they all knew—this was the young man who had rescued the children from the fire.

After a long silence the judge brushed away a tear and cleared his throat. "Son," he said, "your scars show me the depth of your devotion to these children. Because of your great sacrifice, I believe I should award these little ones to you as the reward of your suffering!"

But there is indeed another *Wounded Soldier* who deserves the reward of His suffering. His scars tell the story of what He did for us. Let's return to the scene at Calvary to view again those wounds. But let's focus in on the greatest wound of all. It's the wound in His heart...

All this time on the cross, Jesus' heart has been swelling and filling with grief. The wrath of God has smashed and pummeled Him until His heart is ready to burst. Now with the last drops of the Father cup drained, the cry of forsakenness wrenched from His lips and shot up in His Father's face, His heart begins to crack.

Jesus' tongue is parched from drinking this fiery cup of hell. Now He hangs His head and groans, "I thirst."[1] A Roman soldier wets the Lord's lips with posca, a cheap vinegar wine. Then He lifts His voice and shouts triumphantly, *"Tetelestai!"* In the perfect tense, it means, "It has now and will forever remain finished!"

With the Father's cup of wrath consumed, His work on earth is done. Because sin has been fully punished in Him, demons have no more sin to feed on. Now the "Seed of the woman" crushes the serpents head. It is just as the Bible says, "And having disarmed the powers and authorities, he made a public spectacle of them, triumphing over them by the cross."

Yes, even as God finished His work of creation on the sixth day, Jesus finishes His work of redemption with His sixth word. And then, even as God entered His rest on the seventh day of creation, Jesus enters His rest with His seventh word, "Father, into your hands I commit my spirit."

And now it happens...

His heart breaks. It ruptures, pouring out blood and water.[1] Yes, Jesus dies of a broken heart from the agony of drinking the Father's cup of wrath. Do you know what this means? It's not just the tearing of a veil in heaven. It's the ripping of the veil of the Son of God himself. When the veil in the temple was torn in two from top to bottom, it was symbolic of the tearing of the veil of Jesus' flesh, torn in two so that we could come into the presence of God.

Watch now as a Roman soldier draws back a spear and plunges it into the side of the Lamb. See blood and water flow out separately. His blood is for your cleansing and the water is for your refreshing. They pour from His ruptured heart.

Think of it. God the Son came down from heaven to take your hell, and it ripped His heart in two. Yes, the Olive was crushed to pour out the oil of His love. The grape was pressed to squeeze out His mercy for you. The vase was shattered to release the fragrance of His glory on you. Did you ever know He loved you so much? This is the glory of His love. That's why only at the feet of the Lamb can we really begin to "grasp how wide and long and high and deep is the love of Christ."

So look with me now into a garden tomb. Three days have passed since Jesus was crucified. Darkness still shrouds the land as the Morning Star prepares to rise. Now the Father sends the breath of the Holy Spirit to invade the corpse of His Son.

Jesus takes a breath. His heart begins to beat. Glory pumps through every vein. His eyelids flutter open. And suddenly, the whole tomb floods with the resurrection glory of Christ.

Now the "Sun of Righteousness" rises "with healing in His wings and His beams."[1] The "Dayspring from on high" sheds forth His shining rays. The "light of the world" fills the tomb with His glory.[1] And as Jesus steps out of the tomb in His resurrection body, His flesh is flawless in every way, except for one thing...

Deep, gaping wounds are still cut into His flesh. That's why, when He appears to His disciples that evening, He shows them the holes in hands and feet and side. "Look at my hands and my feet. It is I myself! Touch me and see," He says to His disciples.[1] A week later He says to Thomas, "Put your finger here; see my hands. Reach out

61

your hand and put it into my side. Stop doubting and believe."

Why is He so intent on showing them His wounds? Because He wants us to know that His flesh still bears scars. For though wounds on earth heal with time, and scars in heaven disappear, the scars on Jesus' body never vanish. Forever they remain, carved into His flesh, ever reminding us of His infinite love.

"All scars tell a story," says Dan Stevers. "Ours are stories of pain and brokenness. But God's are a story of forgiveness and healing. And for all eternity His scars will continue to tell a story of God's unending love."

So if ever you doubt His love for you, even as Thomas doubted, simply pause and look up at the *Wounded Soldier* upon the throne. Like the scarred soldier in the opening story of this chapter, His wounds tell a powerful story. He simply lifts up His hands. He says not a word, but the wounds speak for themselves. Loudly they cry, "This is how much I love you!"

Here in America we decorate our soldiers with well-deserved ribbons, and badges, and medals of honor, pinned upon their jackets. Soldiers who show exceptional courage and valor in combat are awarded military decorations such as the Bronze Star, the Silver Star, the Gold Star, the Distinguished Service Cross, and the highest honor of all—the United States Congressional Medal of Honor. Often awarded posthumously, it is given to soldiers of any branch of the Armed Forces who bravely risk their lives and go beyond the call of duty.

But don't forget, there is another *Wounded Soldier* who gave His life and went far beyond the call of duty. Jesus' scars are His medals, embedded into His flesh. They are His ribbons and badges, emblazoned across His body. He was wounded in His head, His hands, His feet, His side, His back and chest.

Most of all He was wounded in His heart, which ruptured when He took the explosion of wrath and hell for you and me. His whole body, inside and out, was decorated with these medals of glory. If anyone deserves to be honored, it's Him. If anyone deserves the reward of His suffering it's Jesus—the most highly decorated *Wounded Soldier* of all!

Chapter Eight: The Soldier's Homecoming

"Why did God allow me to suffer?"

Dave Roever kissed his wife goodbye and said, "Baby, I'll return without a scar." Soon he was shipped off to Vietnam, where one day, while navigating down a dangerous river, tragedy struck. As gunfire exploded from the trees along the river, Dave picked up a white phosphorus grenade, pulled the pin, and drew back his arm to throw it toward an enemy hut. But before he could release the grenade, a sniper's bullet hit it, causing it to explode in his hand.

Dave's whole body was suddenly on fire. He jumped in the river, but water doesn't quench phosphorous fire. Dave's skin kept burning. When he came up, gasping for air, he sucked fire down into his lungs, scorching his bronchial tubes, his vocal cords, and his mouth. "God, I still believe in You!" he groaned as he surfaced from the water.

Dave was left blind in one eye, deaf in one ear, which had been blown off, and the whole right side of his head was burned down to the skull. Medics loaded him onto a stretcher, but he burned right through it, falling and hitting the ground.

Eventually he was transported to Brooke Army Medical Center in San Antonio, Texas. This is where he had seen the selfish young wife flip her wedding ring on her dying husband's bed, walking out on him and breaking his heart (Chapter Six). Because of his hideous wounds she was too ashamed to be seen with him. So naturally, Dave felt anxious about Brenda visiting him. Would she walk out on him like that other wife? He didn't think she would, but still he felt nervous about her coming to visit. What would her reaction be to his homecoming?

On the day of her arrival at the hospital, Brenda was unable to recognize her husband's disfigured body. She had to read the chart on the bed and the tag on his arm to be sure it was him. Convinced it was her husband, she bent down and kissed his marred and bandaged face. "I want you to know that I love you. Welcome home, Dave," she said warmly.

Struggling to speak, he whispered, "I'm sorry, Brenda, that I won't be good-looking anymore." Brenda smiled, "That's okay, Dave, you weren't that good looking in the first place!"

Dave said later, "Wow—the power of true love! As soon as I heard that, it brought a rush of tears to my eyes, and continues to do so each time I repeat the story."

When I hear this story, I want to thank God for all the wives and parents who are caring for their wounded sons and daughters, husbands and wives. I cannot imagine the suffering you are enduring. For those of you who have lost your loved ones in battles overseas, I weep with you in your grief.

And when I think of the sacrifice all of you soldiers have made, I can hardly speak, my heart is so full of emotion. Whether you are in the Air Force, the Amy, the Marine Corps, the Navy, or the Coast Guard, you all deserve our deepest gratitude. Thank you for enduring the heart ache of leaving those you love, your families, your husbands and wives, your children. Thank you for the loneliness of being far from home at Christmas and Thanksgiving and birthdays and graduations and other special family events.

Thank you for stepping up when others stepped down. Thank you for the courage to lay your life on the line to protect us. Thank you for being willing to go into enemy territory to fight to save innocent lives. Thank you for placing yourself in the way of danger to protect others, and for sacrificing everything for the cause of freedom. I am so deeply sorry for those who never tell you how much they appreciate you. Maybe they are like me and just can't express the words without bursting into tears.

Please allow me and countless others to thank you for your sacrificial love. This verse from the Bible describes the extent of your love. "This is how we know what love is: Jesus Christ laid down his life for us.

And we ought to lay down our lives for our brothers."

Now when I think of that moment of reunion for Dave Roever and his wife, I think of all the other husbands and wives, mothers and fathers welcoming home their wounded soldiers. And my thoughts always slip to another reunion—the reunion between the Father and His Wounded Son...

Here He comes—*the Wounded Soldier*—still bearing wounds from His sacrifice on earth. Jesus has come from the battlefield of the cross and now He ascends back to heaven.

The Father waits with outstretched arms, His heart filling with emotion. Such excitement fills the Son that He almost stumbles as He heads straight for His Father's waiting arms. Finally He reaches Him and falls into His trembling embrace. At last *the Wounded Soldier* is home.

When I meditate on this divine homecoming, I can imagine the Father and Son weeping, sobbing, in each other's arm. The Holy Spirit hovers over them, enveloping them in this divine reunion.

Can you picture Him with me? At last the sacrifice of the ages is complete. The work on earth is done. *The Wounded Soldier* has paid the ultimate price. His blood has been shed. Sin has been punished. Satan has been defeated. Hell has been vanquished for those who accept His valiant sacrifice. And salvation for those who will receive Him has been purchased.

When finally the tears in the Godhead subside, I can almost see the Father lifting His arm and pointing toward His Son. "Behold the Lamb, slain from the foundation of the world!" He thunders. And then He surely must have said, with tears trembling in His eyes, "He is forever *My Wounded Soldier Son!*"

No one can know the immeasurable sacrifice this was for the Father. He gave His one and only Son. The agony this brought the Father is unthinkable. Sorrow engulfed His tender heart when He punished His Son in our place. But He did it all for love. He ripped His Son from His side and gave Him as our *Wounded Soldier*. Such amazing love staggers our human understanding.

And yet, all over the world, when people go through hard times, they lift their fists toward heaven and cry, "Why God? Why do you allow such suffering?" Maybe even you have wondered, "Why did God allow me to suffer?"

But this is the wrong question. The question is not "why?" The question is "what?" It is not "why does God allow suffering?" It is "what has God done about human suffering?"

What has God done about the epidemic of sin that ravages the earth, mutilates innocent soldiers, rapes little children, destroys homes, and devastates human lives? What has God done about this disease of sin that pulses through the veins of every human being? His answer is fathomless.[1]

It can be found on a little hill outside Jerusalem. Here on two stakes of wood, the Son of God twisted and thrashed under the hideous weight of sin. Like a raft on a storm tossed sea, He pitched and flailed in agony. Then His body stiffened and His soul endured the horror of God's wrath. As He took the punishment of hell for human sin, He cried out in anguish, "My God, why have you forsaken me?" He was forsaken to save a fallen human race from devastation. "For God so loved the world that He *gave* His one and only Son that whoever believes in him will have everlasting life."

So what is God's answer to human suffering? His answer is stunning. In a word it is this—He gave His one and only Son as *The Wounded Soldier.*

Chapter Nine: The Greatest Soldier

America needs a revelation of the Lamb

Soldiers watch in solemn respect as a long line of United Nations prisoners of war stagger across "Freedom Bridge" at the end of the Korean War. One young man, his eyes dull and his face gray, drags his emaciated body over the bridge. At one point, he stumbles into the railing of the bridge.

Every eye focuses on the bony-armed, stick-like figure of a man, now with lines of suffering scribbled across his face. Rushing to his side an MP Major tries to help, but the gallant soldier waves him away. The soldier's eyes are focused on something ahead. He wants no one to help him reach his goal.

There it is, just across the bridge—held high as a valiant symbol of freedom—the American flag. The young man fixes his eyes on the Stars and Stripes, unfurled in the wind and lifted upon a pole. With every ounce of strength in his body, he hobbles toward the flag.

He shuffles faster now, finally reaching it. Suddenly, he falls to his knees, trembling. He reaches up and tugs at the flag. The flag bearer lowers it and the soldier buries his face in the red and white stripes, sobbing and shaking uncontrollably.

Every man fights to choke back his emotion. Throats tighten, and tears stream down each face. The silence is deafening. Finally, the MP, his cheeks moist with tears, tenderly picks up this skeleton of a young man and carries him to an ambulance.

I know that you who serve in the military understand this kind of patriotism. P.O. W. Colonel Glenn Frazier said to me, "The first thing I did when I stepped onto American soil was to fall down and kiss the ground. Every other soldier behind me did the same."

But how do you feel when you see Americans burning the flag and denigrating this nation? It must make you heart-sick, even sicker than the traumatic scenes of war. You know the blood that has spilled into the ground to keep America free, and yet before our very eyes we see our freedoms slipping away. We see corrupt, power-hungry politicians leading us away from the God-entrusted principles on which this nation was built.

That is why I have written this little book. America needs a revelation of *The Greatest Wounded Soldier* himself to bring us back on course. We need to see Him so that our hearts can melt in true repentance. The massacre on American shores on September 11, 2001 temporarily brought us to our knees, but now pride and complacency and political corruption have settled back into the fabric of this nation. That's why America needs a revelation of the wounded Lamb.

Not until Thomas saw the wounds of the risen Christ did he fall on his knees and cry, "My Lord and my God!"[1] Not until Isaiah saw the Lord did he see his own uncleanness.[1] Not until Job saw God with his spiritual eyes did he genuinely repent in dust and ashes.[1] America needs to see the Lord—*The Greatest Wounded Soldier*—to bring us to our knees in genuine repentance.

Yet many Americans, even Christians, bristle at the mere mention of sin and repentance. Why is that? It is my conviction that the primary reason we have lost heart for repentance is because we have lost sight of *the Wounded Soldier*. We think we know all about the cross, but how deeply have we looked at the wounds, the cries, the cup of wrath Jesus drank? How deeply have we allowed the sacrifice of Christ to pierce us to the core of our hearts? Most of us have cried more tears over the death of our dogs than over the death of our God.

John the Baptist preached his finest sermon the day he pointed to Jesus and cried, "Behold! The Lamb of God!" After this revelation of the Lamb, came his second greatest sermon: "He will baptize you with the Holy Spirit and fire!"[1] America needs a baptism of fire that will sweep the country with revival. We need to look up at *the Wounded Soldier*, seated at the Father's right hand, until heaven opens and revival descends like sparks of fire from the altar above.

We need to feel the hot flecks of revival showering down upon us until the dry tinder of our hearts ignites with blazing revival. As Billy Graham said, a few days after September 11, 2001, "One of the things we desperately need is a spiritual renewal in this country. We need a spiritual revival in America!"

Through the years, revivals have come and gone from the shores of North America. But the primary reason they eventually smoked out is because repentance faded, the gospel ceased being preached, and the cross was no longer lifted. If you will read my book, *The Unquenchable Flame,* you will see that the secret of keeping the fires of revival burning is to keep the cross of Christ central. Historically, this has always been the key to undying flames of revival.

Once you have tasted the sweetness of God's presence in revival, hunger will ache in your soul. Thirst will burn in your being. Having breathed in the rich atmosphere of heaven, your heart will yearn and groan for more and more of Him. You will cry, "Give me revival or I die!"

But will you cry this for America? Rachel cried, "Give me children or I die!" John Knox of Scotland cried, "Give me Scotland or I die!" Will you be one who will lift your voice to heaven and cry, "Give me revival for America or I die!" For our nation needs a revelation of *the Greatest Wounded Soldier* to break us in true repentance and baptize us in revival fire.

America needs her faith regenerated, her passions inflamed, her feelings quickened, her emotions stirred. I'm not talking about emotional*ism,* but true godly feelings that come from the heart of God. We need to have our repentance reawakened, patriotism reestablished, courageous leadership restored, virtuous principles revitalized, hope renewed, love for God rekindled, and revival re-ignited.

God shed His grace on America so that we could shine as a beacon to the world. He wanted us to be a land where men and women of all races would be free to worship Him. The bleeding wounds on the soul of this nation need to be healed. We need repentance and forgiveness to flow until at last racial harmony fills the land. Only a profound revelation of the wounded One can bring us back together.

In every corner of this country— from the glistening lakes in the north, to the gleaming cities of the east, to the fertile plains of the heartland, to the majestic mountains of the west, to the snow-white cotton fields and oil wells of the south, from sea to shining sea—America needs a revelation of *the Greatest Wounded Soldier* of all.

As I wrote in the beginning, a former slave lifted up her little girl, as a train which carried the flag-draped coffin of the fatally wounded Abraham Lincoln passed by. "Take a long look, Honey!" she cried, that's the man who died to set you free!"

In an even higher way we need to call America to take a long deep look at *the Greatest Wounded Soldier* who died to set us free. We need to see heaven open and have a transforming vision of God. In this hour of dying hopes and shattered dreams, as patriotism fades, morals decline, suicides rise, families split, and terrorism infiltrates our shores, this is what we must have.

Indeed, it is high time to inject hope into the bloodstream of our nation.

It's time to transfuse her vessels with the blood drawn from the veins of the Lamb. It's time to call America to look up and see a transforming vision of *the Greatest Wounded Soldier.*

So I challenge those of you, especially humble American soldiers, who still hold dear the values on which this nation was founded, raise up this standard of hope. Give America a revelation of *the Wounded Soldier.* Do it with love bleeding from your heart and passion burning in your words. Call America to turn back to the cross, and speak about it in your own humble way. Because of your sacrificial service, you have earned the right to be heard.

Now as you come to the end of this book, I hope you have felt my heart in these pages. As I said in the beginning, this is my gift of gratitude to you. I hope you have felt my appreciation, my respect, and my tears as you have read.

So I want to close these pages with prayer. First, I want to pray for you; then I want to ask you to join me in a prayer for America, and finally, I will ask you to pray for yourself.

I believe the Holy Spirit is already forging a deep revelation of the cross into your heart, so now I pray for you:

Father, please impart to this hungry one a vision of the Wounded Soldier that will never fade. Let a view of His flowing wounds be forever painted on his or her heart. May a vision of Jesus, drinking His Father's cup and taking our punishment for sin, cause this one's spirit to never cease trembling.

Now I pray, Father, that you will drench this seeking soul with life-giving streams of your presence. Come, Holy Spirit, and pour revival down upon this thirsty one. Soak this longing heart in the healing floods that pour from the Wounded Soldier.

Please open wide and let God fill you with His sweet Holy Spirit. Be forever gripped by the vision of the Lamb, for you can only give to others what He has given you. May you spend the rest of your life calling others to see the Lord. May they behold *the Wounded Soldier* until life-giving rivers from His ruptured heart flow down upon them too.

And now, join me as we cry to God for America:

O God, we plead with you to save America! Forgive us for our pride, our materialism, our immorality, our complacency, our greed, and for allowing corrupt politicians to rule in this land. Christ alone is Lord and King! Help us to become a nation wholly dependent on Him.

Have mercy on our nation, and send revival to America! Let the wound torn open in the side of the Lamb bring floods and floods and more floods of revival to this land. Let your river of revival sweep over this nation and cover this country from sea to shining sea.

One last time, I would like to ask you to kneel down and reach up to touch the wounds in Jesus' hands and feet. Like the emaciated prisoner of war, who stumbled over Freedom Bridge to bury his face into the folds of the Stars and Stripes, reach up and touch the scars and stripes of the ultimate *Wounded Soldier.* Grasp His bleeding hand and let Him feel your heart as you tell Him:

O Lord, it is my highest motive and my deepest passion to bring you the reward of your suffering as a Lamb. For the rest of my life, everything I do will flow out of this grand vision. Until I breathe my last breath, I will lift you up and give America a grand revelation of **the Greatest Wounded Soldier** of all! – Amen.

Ministry Information

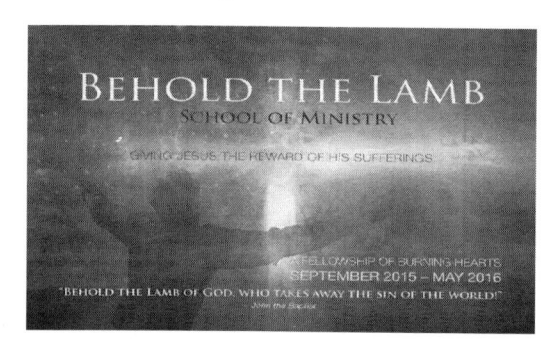

BEHOLD THE LAMB SCHOOL OF MINISTRY (BLSM):

A nine-month mission and ministry training school, launching September 2015

Thundering across the earth, burning in hungry hearts, a movement to "Behold the Lamb of God" has quietly arisen. You are now invited to take part in this fellowship of burning hearts whose highest passion is to bring Jesus, the Lamb who was slain, the reward of His suffering. As you draw close to the Wounded Soldier, your own wounds will be healed, you will be ignited with revival fire, and you will be launched into the harvest field. The Father waits for His Son to be glorified on earth as He is in heaven. Join us for the adventure.

7 Distinctives: *What makes this different from other schools?*

The Revelation of the Lamb, the Wounded Soldier – Bring your heart to the foot of the cross and let it flame with revelation.

Theology Ablaze – Receive a solid foundation in biblical theology that burns.

The Lamb's Heart – Develop a lifestyle of forgiveness, intimacy with God, prayer and worship.

Becoming a Voice – Discover how to preach, write, and communicate with apostolic power and anointing.

Supernatural Evangelism – Go with us into the harvest field to win souls with miracles and the power of the true gospel.

Practical Ministry Experience – Step into opportunities to preach, pray, lead worship, and evangelize.

Mission to the poor – Learn about God's justice, traveling on an international mission to the poor.

Apply for BLSM or internship at www.behold-ministries.org;
email: beholdmininistries@outlook.com

Unquenchable Flame Internships:

If you yearn for revival but cannot attend BLSM, join us in a ten day or two week internship at Evangelist Steve Hill's former home, which has now been made into a beautiful small campground. In just a short time, you will be undone by the sacrifice of Christ on the cross, you will find your preaching voice, develop fervent prayer, evangelize on the beach, and receive impartations of revival fire.

Apply for BLSM, internship or seminar: www.behold-ministries.org or for more information email us: beholdmininistries@outlook.com

Behold & Be Healed Seminar

A weekend seminar on how to receive healing to your heart wounds by beholding the Lamb of God.

Behold & Be Ignited Seminar

A weekend seminar on how to receive the fire of the Holy Spirit and revival by beholding the Lamb of God.

If you would like to contact Dr. Sandy about the book you just read, The Wounded Soldier, please email her at the above address.

Other Books by Dr. Sandy:

The Mystery of Avraham's Lamb
(coming soon)
UNDONE by a Revelation of the Lamb
The Unquenchable Flame
The Pierced Generation
The Glory of the Lamb
Bethlehem's Lamb
Bethlehem's Lamb (Audio Book)
Rivers of Glory
The Masterpiece
A Revelation of the Lamb for America
America Ablaze
India Ablaze
The Pain (booklet)
The Pain in an African Heart (booklet)

Children's Books:

Would Jesus Eat His Vegetables?
How Would Jesus Act at Bedtime?
Would Jesus be a Bad Sport?

To order books, visit us online:
behold-ministries.org/bookstore

Made in the USA
San Bernardino, CA
12 January 2015